INFORMATION

NAME	
ADDRESS	
EMAIL	
PHONE NUMBER	
FAX NUMBER	

LOG BOOK DETAILS

LOG START DATE	
LOG BOOK NUMBER	

INDEX

PAGE NUMBER	SUBJECT
1	
2	
3	
4	
5	
6	
7	
8	
9	
10	
11	
12	
13	
14	
15	
16	
17	
18	
19	
20	
21	
22	
23	
24	
25	
26	
27	
28	
29	
30	

INDEX

PAGE NUMBER	SUBJECT
31	
32	
33	
34	
35	
36	
37	
38	
39	
40	
41	
42	
43	
44	
45	
46	
47	
48	
49	
50	
51	
52	
53	
54	
55	
56	
57	
58	
59	
60	

INDEX

PAGE NUMBER	SUBJECT
61	
62	
63	
64	
65	
66	
67	
68	
69	
70	
71	
72	
73	
74	
75	
76	
77	
78	
79	
80	
81	
82	
83	
84	
85	
86	
87	
88	
89	
90	

INDEX

PAGE NUMBER	SUBJECT
91	
92	
93	
94	
95	
96	
97	
98	
99	
100	
101	
102	
103	
104	
105	
106	
107	
108	
109	
110	
111	
112	
113	
114	
115	
116	
117	
118	
119	
120	

Year :

Month :

Day : | M | T | W | T | F | S | S |

Date :

Department	
Staff Name	Rank / Grade
Supervisor's Name	
Handover Type	
Handover Time	
Handover to (Name)	

Staff No :		Shift :	
Date In :	Time In :	Date Out :	Time Out :

Hours Worked	
Signature	
Job Description :	
Equipment Condition	
Shift Report	

Action to Complete

No.	Action	Completed Date

Completed Actions

No.	Action	Completed Date

NOTES

CLOSING SHIFT SIGNATURE

STARTING SHIFT SIGNATURE

Year : _____

Month : _____

Day :

M	T	W	T	F	S	S

Date : _____

Department	
Staff Name	Rank / Grade
Supervisor's Name	
Handover Type	
Handover Time	
Handover to (Name)	
Staff No :	Shift :
Date In :	Time In :	Date Out :	Time Out :
Hours Worked	
Signature	
Job Description :	
Equipment Condition	
Shift Report	

Action to Complete

No.	Action	Completed Date

Completed Actions

No.	Action	Completed Date

NOTES

_____

CLOSING SHIFT SIGNATURE

STARTING SHIFT SIGNATURE

Year : _____   Month : _____

Day : | M | T | W | T | F | S | S |
|---|---|---|---|---|---|---|
| | | | | | | |

Date : _____

Department			
Staff Name		Rank / Grade	
Supervisor's Name			
Handover Type			
Handover Time			
Handover to (Name)			
Staff No :		Shift :	
Date In :	Time In :	Date Out :	Time Out :
Hours Worked			
Signature			
Job Description :			
Equipment Condition			
Shift Report			

Action to Complete

No.	Action	Completed Date

Completed Actions

No.	Action	Completed Date

NOTES

CLOSING SHIFT SIGNATURE   STARTING SHIFT SIGNATURE

Year :							Month :	

Day :	M	T	W	T	F	S	S		Date :	

Department	
Staff Name	Rank / Grade
Supervisor's Name	
Handover Type	
Handover Time	
Handover to (Name)	

Staff No :		Shift :	
Date In :	Time In :	Date Out :	Time Out :

Hours Worked	
Signature	
Job Description :	
Equipment Condition	
Shift Report	

Action to Complete

No.	Action	Completed Date

Completed Actions

No.	Action	Completed Date

NOTES

_____
CLOSING SHIFT SIGNATURE

_____
STARTING SHIFT SIGNATURE

Year :

Month :

Day : | M | T | W | T | F | S | S |
|---|---|---|---|---|---|---|
| | | | | | | |

Date :

Department	
Staff Name	**Rank / Grade**
Supervisor's Name	
Handover Type	
Handover Time	
Handover to (Name)	
Staff No :	Shift :
Date In :	Time In :	Date Out :	Time Out :
Hours Worked	
Signature	
Job Description :	
Equipment Condition	
Shift Report	

Action to Complete

No.	Action	Completed Date

Completed Actions

No.	Action	Completed Date

NOTES

CLOSING SHIFT SIGNATURE

STARTING SHIFT SIGNATURE

Year :

Month :

Day :

M	T	W	T	F	S	S

Date :

Department	
Staff Name	**Rank / Grade**
Supervisor's Name	
Handover Type	
Handover Time	
Handover to (Name)	
Staff No :	**Shift :**
Date In :	**Time In :** **Date Out :** **Time Out :**
Hours Worked	
Signature	
Job Description :	
Equipment Condition	
Shift Report	

Action to Complete

No.	Action	Completed Date

Completed Actions

No.	Action	Completed Date

NOTES

CLOSING SHIFT SIGNATURE　　　**STARTING SHIFT SIGNATURE**

Year :

Month :

Day : | M | T | W | T | F | S | S |
|---|---|---|---|---|---|---|
| | | | | | | |

Date :

Department	
Staff Name	Rank / Grade
Supervisor's Name	
Handover Type	
Handover Time	
Handover to (Name)	
Staff No :	Shift :
Date In :	Time In : Date Out : Time Out :
Hours Worked	
Signature	
Job Description :	
Equipment Condition	
Shift Report	

Action to Complete

No.	Action	Completed Date

Completed Actions

No.	Action	Completed Date

NOTES

CLOSING SHIFT SIGNATURE

STARTING SHIFT SIGNATURE

Year :

Day : | M | T | W | T | F | S | S |
|---|---|---|---|---|---|---|
| | | | | | | |

Month :

Date :

Department	
Staff Name	**Rank / Grade**
Supervisor's Name	
Handover Type	
Handover Time	
Handover to (Name)	
Staff No :	**Shift :**
Date In : Time In :	Date Out : Time Out :
Hours Worked	
Signature	
Job Description :	
Equipment Condition	
Shift Report	

Action to Complete

No.	Action	Completed Date

Completed Actions

No.	Action	Completed Date

NOTES

_____

CLOSING SHIFT SIGNATURE   **STARTING SHIFT SIGNATURE**

Year :

Month :

Day :

M	T	W	T	F	S	S

Date :

Department	
Staff Name	**Rank / Grade**
Supervisor's Name	
Handover Type	
Handover Time	
Handover to (Name)	
Staff No :	**Shift :**
Date In :	**Time In :** **Date Out :** **Time Out :**
Hours Worked	
Signature	
Job Description :	
Equipment Condition	
Shift Report	

Action to Complete

No.	Action	Completed Date

Completed Actions

No.	Action	Completed Date

NOTES

CLOSING SHIFT SIGNATURE

STARTING SHIFT SIGNATURE

Year :

Month :

Day :

M	T	W	T	F	S	S

Date :

Department	
Staff Name	**Rank / Grade**
Supervisor's Name	
Handover Type	
Handover Time	
Handover to (Name)	
Staff No :	**Shift :**
Date In :	**Time In :** **Date Out :** **Time Out :**
Hours Worked	
Signature	
Job Description :	
Equipment Condition	
Shift Report	

Action to Complete

No.	Action	Completed Date

Completed Actions

No.	Action	Completed Date

NOTES

CLOSING SHIFT SIGNATURE

STARTING SHIFT SIGNATURE

Year :							Month :	
Day :	M	T	W	T	F	S	S	Date :

Department	
Staff Name	Rank / Grade
Supervisor's Name	
Handover Type	
Handover Time	
Handover to (Name)	
Staff No :	Shift :
Date In :	Time In :	Date Out :	Time Out :
Hours Worked	
Signature	
Job Description :	
Equipment Condition	
Shift Report	

Action to Complete

No.	Action	Completed Date

Completed Actions

No.	Action	Completed Date

NOTES

CLOSING SHIFT SIGNATURE

STARTING SHIFT SIGNATURE

Year : _____

Month : _____

Day : | M | T | W | T | F | S | S |
|---|---|---|---|---|---|---|
| | | | | | | |

Date : _____

Department	
Staff Name	Rank / Grade
Supervisor's Name	
Handover Type	
Handover Time	
Handover to (Name)	
Staff No :	Shift :
Date In :	Time In :	Date Out :	Time Out :
Hours Worked	
Signature	
Job Description :	
Equipment Condition	
Shift Report	

Action to Complete

No.	Action	Completed Date

Completed Actions

No.	Action	Completed Date

NOTES

_____

CLOSING SHIFT SIGNATURE   **STARTING SHIFT SIGNATURE**

Year : _____

Month : _____

Day :

M	T	W	T	F	S	S

Date : _____

Department	
Staff Name		**Rank / Grade**	
Supervisor's Name	
Handover Type	
Handover Time	
Handover to (Name)	
Staff No :		**Shift :**
Date In :	**Time In :**	**Date Out :**	**Time Out :**
Hours Worked	
Signature	
Job Description :	
Equipment Condition	
Shift Report	

Action to Complete

No.	Action	Completed Date

Completed Actions

No.	Action	Completed Date

NOTES

_____

_____

_____

_____

_____

_____

_____   _____
CLOSING SHIFT SIGNATURE   **STARTING SHIFT SIGNATURE**

Year :

Month :

Day :

M	T	W	T	F	S	S

Date :

Department	
Staff Name	**Rank / Grade**
Supervisor's Name	
Handover Type	
Handover Time	
Handover to (Name)	
Staff No :	**Shift :**
Date In :	**Time In :** / **Date Out :** / **Time Out :**
Hours Worked	
Signature	
Job Description :	
Equipment Condition	
Shift Report	

Action to Complete

No.	Action	Completed Date

Completed Actions

No.	Action	Completed Date

NOTES

CLOSING SHIFT SIGNATURE

STARTING SHIFT SIGNATURE

Year :

Month :

Day :

M	T	W	T	F	S	S

Date :

Department	
Staff Name	**Rank / Grade**
Supervisor's Name	
Handover Type	
Handover Time	
Handover to (Name)	
Staff No :	**Shift :**
Date In :	**Time In :** **Date Out :** **Time Out :**
Hours Worked	
Signature	
Job Description :	
Equipment Condition	
Shift Report	

Action to Complete

No.	Action	Completed Date

Completed Actions

No.	Action	Completed Date

NOTES

_____
CLOSING SHIFT SIGNATURE

_____
STARTING SHIFT SIGNATURE

Year :

Day : | M | T | W | T | F | S | S |
|---|---|---|---|---|---|---|
| | | | | | | |

Month :

Date :

Department	
Staff Name	Rank / Grade
Supervisor's Name	
Handover Type	
Handover Time	
Handover to (Name)	
Staff No :	Shift :
Date In :	Time In :	Date Out :	Time Out :
Hours Worked	
Signature	
Job Description :	
Equipment Condition	
Shift Report	

Action to Complete

No.	Action	Completed Date

Completed Actions

No.	Action	Completed Date

NOTES

CLOSING SHIFT SIGNATURE   STARTING SHIFT SIGNATURE

Year :								Month :	

Day :	M	T	W	T	F	S	S		Date :	

Department	
Staff Name	Rank / Grade
Supervisor's Name	
Handover Type	
Handover Time	
Handover to (Name)	
Staff No :	Shift :
Date In :	Time In :	Date Out :	Time Out :
Hours Worked	
Signature	
Job Description :	
Equipment Condition	
Shift Report	

Action to Complete

No.	Action	Completed Date

Completed Actions

No.	Action	Completed Date

NOTES

CLOSING SHIFT SIGNATURE   STARTING SHIFT SIGNATURE

Year :

Day : | M | T | W | T | F | S | S |
|---|---|---|---|---|---|---|
| | | | | | | |

Month :

Date :

Department	
Staff Name	**Rank / Grade**
Supervisor's Name	
Handover Type	
Handover Time	
Handover to (Name)	
Staff No :	**Shift :**
Date In :	Time In :	**Date Out :**	Time Out :
Hours Worked	
Signature	
Job Description :	
Equipment Condition	
Shift Report	

Action to Complete

No.	Action	Completed Date

Completed Actions

No.	Action	Completed Date

NOTES

CLOSING SHIFT SIGNATURE

STARTING SHIFT SIGNATURE

Year :

Day : | M | T | W | T | F | S | S |
| | | | | | | |

Month :

Date :

Department	
Staff Name		**Rank / Grade**	
Supervisor's Name	
Handover Type	
Handover Time	
Handover to (Name)	
Staff No :		**Shift :**
Date In :	**Time In :**	**Date Out :**	**Time Out :**
Hours Worked	
Signature	
Job Description :	
Equipment Condition	
Shift Report	

Action to Complete			**Completed Actions**		
No.	Action	Completed Date	No.	Action	Completed Date

NOTES

_____ _____
CLOSING SHIFT SIGNATURE   **STARTING SHIFT SIGNATURE**

Year :

Day : | M | T | W | T | F | S | S |

Month :

Date :

Department	
Staff Name		Rank / Grade	
Supervisor's Name	
Handover Type	
Handover Time	
Handover to (Name)	
Staff No :		Shift :	
Date In :	Time In :	Date Out :	Time Out :
Hours Worked	
Signature	
Job Description :	
Equipment Condition	
Shift Report	

Action to Complete

No.	Action	Completed Date

Completed Actions

No.	Action	Completed Date

NOTES

CLOSING SHIFT SIGNATURE

STARTING SHIFT SIGNATURE

Year :

Day : | M | T | W | T | F | S | S |

Month :

Date :

Department	
Staff Name	Rank / Grade
Supervisor's Name	
Handover Type	
Handover Time	
Handover to (Name)	
Staff No :	Shift :
Date In :	Time In :	Date Out :	Time Out :
Hours Worked	
Signature	
Job Description :	
Equipment Condition	
Shift Report	

Action to Complete

No.	Action	Completed Date

Completed Actions

No.	Action	Completed Date

NOTES

CLOSING SHIFT SIGNATURE

STARTING SHIFT SIGNATURE

Year :

Day : | M | T | W | T | F | S | S |
|---|---|---|---|---|---|---|
| | | | | | | |

Month :

Date :

Department	
Staff Name	Rank / Grade
Supervisor's Name	
Handover Type	
Handover Time	
Handover to (Name)	
Staff No :	Shift :
Date In :	Time In :	Date Out :	Time Out :
Hours Worked	
Signature	
Job Description :	
Equipment Condition	
Shift Report	

Action to Complete

No.	Action	Completed Date

Completed Actions

No.	Action	Completed Date

NOTES

_____
CLOSING SHIFT SIGNATURE

_____
STARTING SHIFT SIGNATURE

Year :

Month :

Day : | M | T | W | T | F | S | S |
|---|---|---|---|---|---|---|
| | | | | | | |

Date :

Department	
Staff Name	Rank / Grade
Supervisor's Name	
Handover Type	
Handover Time	
Handover to (Name)	
Staff No :	Shift :
Date In :	Time In :	Date Out :	Time Out :
Hours Worked	
Signature	
Job Description :	
Equipment Condition	
Shift Report	

Action to Complete

No.	Action	Completed Date

Completed Actions

No.	Action	Completed Date

NOTES

CLOSING SHIFT SIGNATURE

STARTING SHIFT SIGNATURE

Year :

Month :

Day :

M	T	W	T	F	S	S

Date :

Department	
Staff Name	**Rank / Grade**
Supervisor's Name	
Handover Type	
Handover Time	
Handover to (Name)	
Staff No :	**Shift :**
Date In : Time In :	**Date Out :** Time Out :
Hours Worked	
Signature	
Job Description :	
Equipment Condition	
Shift Report	

Action to Complete

No.	Action	Completed Date

Completed Actions

No.	Action	Completed Date

— NOTES —

CLOSING SHIFT SIGNATURE

STARTING SHIFT SIGNATURE

Year : _____

Month : _____

Day : | M | T | W | T | F | S | S |
|---|---|---|---|---|---|---|
| | | | | | | |

Date : _____

Department	
Staff Name	Rank / Grade
Supervisor's Name	
Handover Type	
Handover Time	
Handover to (Name)	
Staff No :	Shift :
Date In :	Time In :	Date Out :	Time Out :
Hours Worked	
Signature	
Job Description :	
Equipment Condition	
Shift Report	

Action to Complete

No.	Action	Completed Date

Completed Actions

No.	Action	Completed Date

NOTES

_____

_____

_____

_____

_____

CLOSING SHIFT SIGNATURE

STARTING SHIFT SIGNATURE

Year : _____

Month : _____

Day :

M	T	W	T	F	S	S

Date : _____

Department	
Staff Name	**Rank / Grade**
Supervisor's Name	
Handover Type	
Handover Time	
Handover to (Name)	
Staff No :	**Shift :**
Date In :	Time In : / Date Out : / Time Out :
Hours Worked	
Signature	
Job Description :	
Equipment Condition	
Shift Report	

Action to Complete

No.	Action	Completed Date

Completed Actions

No.	Action	Completed Date

NOTES

_____

CLOSING SHIFT SIGNATURE   STARTING SHIFT SIGNATURE

Year :

Month :

Day : | M | T | W | T | F | S | S |
|---|---|---|---|---|---|---|
| | | | | | | |

Date :

Department	
Staff Name	Rank / Grade	
Supervisor's Name	
Handover Type	
Handover Time	
Handover to (Name)	
Staff No :	Shift :
Date In :	Time In :	Date Out :	Time Out :
Hours Worked	
Signature	
Job Description :	
Equipment Condition	
Shift Report	

Action to Complete

No.	Action	Completed Date

Completed Actions

No.	Action	Completed Date

NOTES

CLOSING SHIFT SIGNATURE

STARTING SHIFT SIGNATURE

Year :

Month :

Day : | M | T | W | T | F | S | S |
|---|---|---|---|---|---|---|
| | | | | | | |

Date :

Department	
Staff Name	Rank / Grade
Supervisor's Name	
Handover Type	
Handover Time	
Handover to (Name)	
Staff No :	Shift :
Date In :	Time In :	Date Out :	Time Out :
Hours Worked	
Signature	
Job Description :	
Equipment Condition	
Shift Report	

Action to Complete

No.	Action	Completed Date

Completed Actions

No.	Action	Completed Date

NOTES

_____

CLOSING SHIFT SIGNATURE

_____

STARTING SHIFT SIGNATURE

Year : _____

Day :

M	T	W	T	F	S	S

Month : _____

Date : _____

Department	
Staff Name	Rank / Grade
Supervisor's Name	
Handover Type	
Handover Time	
Handover to (Name)	
Staff No :	Shift :
Date In :	Time In :	Date Out :	Time Out :
Hours Worked	
Signature	
Job Description :	
Equipment Condition	
Shift Report	

Action to Complete

No.	Action	Completed Date

Completed Actions

No.	Action	Completed Date

NOTES

_____
_____
_____
_____
_____

CLOSING SHIFT SIGNATURE

STARTING SHIFT SIGNATURE

Year :		Month :	
Day : M T W T F S S		Date :	

Department	
Staff Name	Rank / Grade
Supervisor's Name	
Handover Type	
Handover Time	
Handover to (Name)	
Staff No :	Shift :
Date In :	Time In :	Date Out :	Time Out :
Hours Worked	
Signature	
Job Description :	
Equipment Condition	
Shift Report	

Action to Complete

No.	Action	Completed Date

Completed Actions

No.	Action	Completed Date

NOTES

CLOSING SHIFT SIGNATURE   STARTING SHIFT SIGNATURE

Year :

Month :

Day : | M | T | W | T | F | S | S |

Date :

Department	
Staff Name	Rank / Grade
Supervisor's Name	
Handover Type	
Handover Time	
Handover to (Name)	
Staff No :	Shift :
Date In :	Time In :	Date Out :	Time Out :
Hours Worked	
Signature	
Job Description :	
Equipment Condition	
Shift Report	

Action to Complete

No.	Action	Completed Date

Completed Actions

No.	Action	Completed Date

NOTES

CLOSING SHIFT SIGNATURE

STARTING SHIFT SIGNATURE

Year :

Month :

Day : | M | T | W | T | F | S | S |
| | | | | | | | |

Date :

Department	
Staff Name		Rank / Grade	
Supervisor's Name	
Handover Type	
Handover Time	
Handover to (Name)	
Staff No :		Shift :	
Date In :	Time In :	Date Out :	Time Out :
Hours Worked	
Signature	
Job Description :	
Equipment Condition	
Shift Report	

Action to Complete

No.	Action	Completed Date

Completed Actions

No.	Action	Completed Date

NOTES

CLOSING SHIFT SIGNATURE

STARTING SHIFT SIGNATURE

Year : _____   **Month :** _____

Day :

M	T	W	T	F	S	S

Date : _____

Department	
Staff Name	**Rank / Grade**
Supervisor's Name	
Handover Type	
Handover Time	
Handover to (Name)	
Staff No :	**Shift :**
Date In : Time In :	**Date Out :** Time Out :
Hours Worked	
Signature	
Job Description :	
Equipment Condition	
Shift Report	

Action to Complete

No.	Action	Completed Date

Completed Actions

No.	Action	Completed Date

NOTES

_____
_____
_____
_____
_____
_____
_____

CLOSING SHIFT SIGNATURE   **STARTING SHIFT SIGNATURE**

HANDOVER LOG

34

Year :

Month :

Day : | M | T | W | T | F | S | S |

Date :

Department	
Staff Name	Rank / Grade
Supervisor's Name	
Handover Type	
Handover Time	
Handover to (Name)	

Staff No :   Shift :

Date In :   Time In :   Date Out :   Time Out :

Hours Worked	
Signature	
Job Description :	
Equipment Condition	
Shift Report	

Action to Complete

No.	Action	Completed Date

Completed Actions

No.	Action	Completed Date

NOTES

_____
CLOSING SHIFT SIGNATURE

_____
STARTING SHIFT SIGNATURE

Year : _____

Day :

M	T	W	T	F	S	S

Month : _____

Date : _____

Department	
Staff Name	**Rank / Grade**
Supervisor's Name	
Handover Type	
Handover Time	
Handover to (Name)	
Staff No :	**Shift :**
Date In :	Time In :	Date Out :	Time Out :
Hours Worked	
Signature	
Job Description :	
Equipment Condition	
Shift Report	

Action to Complete

No.	Action	Completed Date

Completed Actions

No.	Action	Completed Date

NOTES

_____
CLOSING SHIFT SIGNATURE

_____
STARTING SHIFT SIGNATURE

Year :

Month :

Day :

M	T	W	T	F	S	S

Date :

Department	
Staff Name	**Rank / Grade**
Supervisor's Name	
Handover Type	
Handover Time	
Handover to (Name)	
Staff No :	**Shift :**
Date In :	**Time In :** / **Date Out :** / **Time Out :**
Hours Worked	
Signature	
Job Description :	
Equipment Condition	
Shift Report	

Action to Complete

No.	Action	Completed Date

Completed Actions

No.	Action	Completed Date

NOTES

CLOSING SHIFT SIGNATURE

STARTING SHIFT SIGNATURE

Year :

Day : | M | T | W | T | F | S | S |
|---|---|---|---|---|---|---|
| | | | | | | |

Month :

Date :

Department	
Staff Name	Rank / Grade
Supervisor's Name	
Handover Type	
Handover Time	
Handover to (Name)	
Staff No :	Shift :
Date In : Time In :	Date Out : Time Out :
Hours Worked	
Signature	
Job Description :	
Equipment Condition	
Shift Report	

Action to Complete

No.	Action	Completed Date

Completed Actions

No.	Action	Completed Date

NOTES

CLOSING SHIFT SIGNATURE

STARTING SHIFT SIGNATURE

Year : _____

Month : _____

Day : | M | T | W | T | F | S | S |
|---|---|---|---|---|---|---|
| | | | | | | |

Date : _____

Department	
Staff Name	Rank / Grade	
Supervisor's Name	
Handover Type	
Handover Time	
Handover to (Name)	
Staff No :	Shift :
Date In :	Time In :	Date Out :	Time Out :
Hours Worked	
Signature	
Job Description :	
Equipment Condition	
Shift Report	

Action to Complete

No.	Action	Completed Date

Completed Actions

No.	Action	Completed Date

NOTES

_____

CLOSING SHIFT SIGNATURE

_____

STARTING SHIFT SIGNATURE

Year :

Day : | M | T | W | T | F | S | S |

Month :

Date :

Department	
Staff Name	Rank / Grade
Supervisor's Name	
Handover Type	
Handover Time	
Handover to (Name)	
Staff No :	Shift :
Date In :	Time In :	Date Out :	Time Out :
Hours Worked	
Signature	
Job Description :	
Equipment Condition	
Shift Report	

Action to Complete

No.	Action	Completed Date

Completed Actions

No.	Action	Completed Date

NOTES

CLOSING SHIFT SIGNATURE   **STARTING SHIFT SIGNATURE**

Year :

Day : | M | T | W | T | F | S | S |
|---|---|---|---|---|---|---|
| | | | | | | |

Month :

Date :

Department	
Staff Name	Rank / Grade
Supervisor's Name	
Handover Type	
Handover Time	
Handover to (Name)	
Staff No :	Shift :
Date In :	Time In :	Date Out :	Time Out :
Hours Worked	
Signature	
Job Description :	
Equipment Condition	
Shift Report	

Action to Complete

No.	Action	Completed Date

Completed Actions

No.	Action	Completed Date

NOTES

CLOSING SHIFT SIGNATURE

STARTING SHIFT SIGNATURE

| Year : | | Month : | |
| Day : M T W T F S S | | Date : | |

Department	
Staff Name	Rank / Grade
Supervisor's Name	
Handover Type	
Handover Time	
Handover to (Name)	
Staff No :	Shift :
Date In :	Time In :	Date Out :	Time Out :
Hours Worked	
Signature	
Job Description :	
Equipment Condition	
Shift Report	

Action to Complete

No.	Action	Completed Date

Completed Actions

No.	Action	Completed Date

NOTES

CLOSING SHIFT SIGNATURE

STARTING SHIFT SIGNATURE

Year :

Day : | M | T | W | T | F | S | S |

Month :

Date :

Department	
Staff Name	

Rank / Grade

Supervisor's Name	
Handover Type	
Handover Time	
Handover to (Name)	
Staff No :	

Shift :

Date In : | **Time In :** | **Date Out :** | **Time Out :** |

Hours Worked	
Signature	
Job Description :	
Equipment Condition	
Shift Report	

Action to Complete

No.	Action	Completed Date

Completed Actions

No.	Action	Completed Date

NOTES

CLOSING SHIFT SIGNATURE

STARTING SHIFT SIGNATURE

Year : [   ]

Month : [   ]

Day :

M	T	W	T	F	S	S

Date : [   ]

Department	
Staff Name	Rank / Grade	
Supervisor's Name	
Handover Type	
Handover Time	
Handover to (Name)	
Staff No :	Shift :
Date In :	Time In :	Date Out :	Time Out :
Hours Worked	
Signature	
Job Description :	
Equipment Condition	
Shift Report	

Action to Complete

No.	Action	Completed Date

Completed Actions

No.	Action	Completed Date

NOTES

CLOSING SHIFT SIGNATURE

STARTING SHIFT SIGNATURE

Year :								Month :	

Day :	M	T	W	T	F	S	S	Date :	

Department	
Staff Name	Rank / Grade
Supervisor's Name	
Handover Type	
Handover Time	
Handover to (Name)	

Staff No :		Shift :	
Date In :	Time In :	Date Out :	Time Out :

Hours Worked	
Signature	
Job Description :	
Equipment Condition	
Shift Report	

Action to Complete

No.	Action	Completed Date

Completed Actions

No.	Action	Completed Date

NOTES

CLOSING SHIFT SIGNATURE   STARTING SHIFT SIGNATURE

Year :

Day : | M | T | W | T | F | S | S |
| | | | | | | |

Month :

Date :

Department	
Staff Name		Rank / Grade	
Supervisor's Name	
Handover Type	
Handover Time	
Handover to (Name)	

Staff No :		Shift :	
Date In :	Time In :	Date Out :	Time Out :
Hours Worked	
Signature	
Job Description :	
Equipment Condition	
Shift Report	

Action to Complete

No.	Action	Completed Date

Completed Actions

No.	Action	Completed Date

NOTES

_____
CLOSING SHIFT SIGNATURE

STARTING SHIFT SIGNATURE

Year :

Day : | M | T | W | T | F | S | S |

Month :

Date :

Department	
Staff Name	Rank / Grade
Supervisor's Name	
Handover Type	
Handover Time	
Handover to (Name)	
Staff No :	Shift :
Date In :	Time In :	Date Out :	Time Out :
Hours Worked	
Signature	
Job Description :	
Equipment Condition	
Shift Report	

Action to Complete

No.	Action	Completed Date

Completed Actions

No.	Action	Completed Date

NOTES

CLOSING SHIFT SIGNATURE

STARTING SHIFT SIGNATURE

Year : _____

Month : _____

Day :

M	T	W	T	F	S	S

Date : _____

Department	
Staff Name	**Rank / Grade**
Supervisor's Name	
Handover Type	
Handover Time	
Handover to (Name)	
Staff No :	**Shift :**
Date In :	**Time In :** **Date Out :** **Time Out :**
Hours Worked	
Signature	
Job Description :	
Equipment Condition	
Shift Report	

Action to Complete

No.	Action	Completed Date

Completed Actions

No.	Action	Completed Date

NOTES

_____

CLOSING SHIFT SIGNATURE   **STARTING SHIFT SIGNATURE**

Year : _____

Month : _____

Day : | M | T | W | T | F | S | S |
|---|---|---|---|---|---|---|
| | | | | | | |

Date : _____

Department	
Staff Name		Rank / Grade	
Supervisor's Name	
Handover Type	
Handover Time	
Handover to (Name)	
Staff No :		Shift :
Date In :	Time In :	Date Out :	Time Out :
Hours Worked	
Signature	
Job Description :	
Equipment Condition	
Shift Report	

Action to Complete

No.	Action	Completed Date

Completed Actions

No.	Action	Completed Date

NOTES

_____

CLOSING SHIFT SIGNATURE

_____

STARTING SHIFT SIGNATURE

Year :

Month :

Day :

M	T	W	T	F	S	S

Date :

Department	
Staff Name	Rank / Grade
Supervisor's Name	
Handover Type	
Handover Time	
Handover to (Name)	

Staff No :		Shift :	

Date In :	Time In :	Date Out :	Time Out :

Hours Worked	
Signature	
Job Description :	
Equipment Condition	
Shift Report	

Action to Complete

No.	Action	Completed Date

Completed Actions

No.	Action	Completed Date

NOTES

CLOSING SHIFT SIGNATURE

STARTING SHIFT SIGNATURE

Year :

Day : | M | T | W | T | F | S | S |

Month :

Date :

Department	
Staff Name	Rank / Grade
Supervisor's Name	
Handover Type	
Handover Time	
Handover to (Name)	
Staff No :	Shift :
Date In :	Time In :	Date Out :	Time Out :
Hours Worked	
Signature	
Job Description :	
Equipment Condition	
Shift Report	

Action to Complete

No.	Action	Completed Date

Completed Actions

No.	Action	Completed Date

NOTES

CLOSING SHIFT SIGNATURE

STARTING SHIFT SIGNATURE

Year :

Day : | M | T | W | T | F | S | S |

Month :

Date :

Department	
Staff Name	Rank / Grade
Supervisor's Name	
Handover Type	
Handover Time	
Handover to (Name)	

Staff No : **Shift :**

Date In : **Time In :** **Date Out :** **Time Out :**

Hours Worked	
Signature	
Job Description :	
Equipment Condition	
Shift Report	

Action to Complete

No.	Action	Completed Date

Completed Actions

No.	Action	Completed Date

NOTES

CLOSING SHIFT SIGNATURE   **STARTING SHIFT SIGNATURE**

Year :

Day : | M | T | W | T | F | S | S |

Month :

Date :

Department	
Staff Name		Rank / Grade	
Supervisor's Name	
Handover Type	
Handover Time	
Handover to (Name)	
Staff No :		Shift :	
Date In :	Time In :	Date Out :	Time Out :
Hours Worked	
Signature	
Job Description :	
Equipment Condition	
Shift Report	

Action to Complete

No.	Action	Completed Date

Completed Actions

No.	Action	Completed Date

NOTES

_____
CLOSING SHIFT SIGNATURE

_____
STARTING SHIFT SIGNATURE

Year :

Month :

Day :

M	T	W	T	F	S	S

Date :

Department	
Staff Name	Rank / Grade
Supervisor's Name	
Handover Type	
Handover Time	
Handover to (Name)	
Staff No :	Shift :
Date In : Time In :	Date Out : Time Out :
Hours Worked	
Signature	
Job Description :	
Equipment Condition	
Shift Report	

Action to Complete

No.	Action	Completed Date

Completed Actions

No.	Action	Completed Date

— NOTES —

CLOSING SHIFT SIGNATURE

STARTING SHIFT SIGNATURE

Year :								Month :	
Day :	M	T	W	T	F	S	S	Date :	

Department	
Staff Name	Rank / Grade
Supervisor's Name	
Handover Type	
Handover Time	
Handover to (Name)	
Staff No :	Shift :
Date In :	Time In : Date Out : Time Out :
Hours Worked	
Signature	
Job Description :	
Equipment Condition	
Shift Report	

Action to Complete

No.	Action	Completed Date

Completed Actions

No.	Action	Completed Date

NOTES

CLOSING SHIFT SIGNATURE   STARTING SHIFT SIGNATURE

Year :							Month :	

Day :	M	T	W	T	F	S	S

Date :

Department	
Staff Name	Rank / Grade
Supervisor's Name	
Handover Type	
Handover Time	
Handover to (Name)	
Staff No :	Shift :
Date In :	Time In :	Date Out :	Time Out :
Hours Worked	
Signature	
Job Description :	
Equipment Condition	
Shift Report	

Action to Complete

No.	Action	Completed Date

Completed Actions

No.	Action	Completed Date

NOTES

CLOSING SHIFT SIGNATURE

STARTING SHIFT SIGNATURE

| Year : | | Month : | |

Day : | M | T | W | T | F | S | S |

Date : | |

Department	
Staff Name		Rank / Grade	
Supervisor's Name	
Handover Type	
Handover Time	
Handover to (Name)	
Staff No :		Shift :	
Date In :	Time In :	Date Out :	Time Out :
Hours Worked	
Signature	
Job Description :	
Equipment Condition	
Shift Report	

Action to Complete

No.	Action	Completed Date

Completed Actions

No.	Action	Completed Date

NOTES

_____ CLOSING SHIFT SIGNATURE

_____ STARTING SHIFT SIGNATURE

Year :

Month :

Day :

M	T	W	T	F	S	S

Date :

Department	
Staff Name	**Rank / Grade**
Supervisor's Name	
Handover Type	
Handover Time	
Handover to (Name)	
Staff No :	Shift :
Date In :	Time In : Date Out : Time Out :
Hours Worked	
Signature	
Job Description :	
Equipment Condition	
Shift Report	

Action to Complete

No.	Action	Completed Date

Completed Actions

No.	Action	Completed Date

NOTES

CLOSING SHIFT SIGNATURE

STARTING SHIFT SIGNATURE

Year :

Month :

Day : | M | T | W | T | F | S | S |
|---|---|---|---|---|---|---|
| | | | | | | |

Date :

Department	
Staff Name	Rank / Grade
Supervisor's Name	
Handover Type	
Handover Time	
Handover to (Name)	
Staff No :	Shift :
Date In : Time In :	Date Out : Time Out :
Hours Worked	
Signature	
Job Description :	
Equipment Condition	
Shift Report	

Action to Complete

No.	Action	Completed Date

Completed Actions

No.	Action	Completed Date

NOTES

CLOSING SHIFT SIGNATURE

STARTING SHIFT SIGNATURE

Year :

Day : | M | T | W | T | F | S | S |
|---|---|---|---|---|---|---|
| | | | | | | |

Month :

Date :

Department	
Staff Name	Rank / Grade
Supervisor's Name	
Handover Type	
Handover Time	
Handover to (Name)	
Staff No :	Shift :
Date In :	Time In :	Date Out :	Time Out :
Hours Worked	
Signature	
Job Description :	
Equipment Condition	
Shift Report	

Action to Complete

No.	Action	Completed Date

Completed Actions

No.	Action	Completed Date

NOTES

CLOSING SHIFT SIGNATURE   **STARTING SHIFT SIGNATURE**

Year :

Day :

M	T	W	T	F	S	S

Month :

Date :

Department	
Staff Name		**Rank / Grade**	
Supervisor's Name	
Handover Type	
Handover Time	
Handover to (Name)	
Staff No :		**Shift :**	
Date In :	**Time In :**	**Date Out :**	**Time Out :**
Hours Worked	
Signature	
Job Description :	
Equipment Condition	
Shift Report	

Action to Complete

No.	Action	Completed Date

Completed Actions

No.	Action	Completed Date

NOTES

CLOSING SHIFT SIGNATURE

STARTING SHIFT SIGNATURE

Year :

Month :

Day :

M	T	W	T	F	S	S

Date :

Department	
Staff Name	**Rank / Grade**
Supervisor's Name	
Handover Type	
Handover Time	
Handover to (Name)	
Staff No :	**Shift :**
Date In : Time In :	**Date Out :** Time Out :
Hours Worked	
Signature	
Job Description :	
Equipment Condition	
Shift Report	

Action to Complete

No.	Action	Completed Date

Completed Actions

No.	Action	Completed Date

NOTES

CLOSING SHIFT SIGNATURE

STARTING SHIFT SIGNATURE

Year :		Month :	

Day :	M	T	W	T	F	S	S	Date :	

Department	
Staff Name		Rank / Grade	
Supervisor's Name	
Handover Type	
Handover Time	
Handover to (Name)	

Staff No :		Shift :	
Date In :	Time In :	Date Out :	Time Out :

Hours Worked	
Signature	
Job Description :	
Equipment Condition	
Shift Report	

Action to Complete

No.	Action	Completed Date

Completed Actions

No.	Action	Completed Date

NOTES

CLOSING SHIFT SIGNATURE   STARTING SHIFT SIGNATURE

Year : _____

Month : _____

Day : | M | T | W | T | F | S | S |
|---|---|---|---|---|---|---|
| | | | | | | |

Date : _____

Department	
Staff Name	Rank / Grade
Supervisor's Name	
Handover Type	
Handover Time	
Handover to (Name)	
Staff No :	Shift :
Date In :	Time In :	Date Out :	Time Out :
Hours Worked	
Signature	
Job Description :	
Equipment Condition	
Shift Report	

Action to Complete

No.	Action	Completed Date

Completed Actions

No.	Action	Completed Date

NOTES

_____

CLOSING SHIFT SIGNATURE

STARTING SHIFT SIGNATURE

Year :

Day :

M	T	W	T	F	S	S

Month :

Date :

Department	
Staff Name	**Rank / Grade**	
Supervisor's Name	
Handover Type	
Handover Time	
Handover to (Name)	
Staff No :	**Shift :**
Date In :	**Time In :**	**Date Out :**	**Time Out :**
Hours Worked	
Signature	
Job Description :	
Equipment Condition	
Shift Report	

Action to Complete

No.	Action	Completed Date

Completed Actions

No.	Action	Completed Date

NOTES

_____

CLOSING SHIFT SIGNATURE

STARTING SHIFT SIGNATURE

Year : _____ Month : _____

Day : | M | T | W | T | F | S | S |

Date : _____

Department	
Staff Name	Rank / Grade
Supervisor's Name	
Handover Type	
Handover Time	
Handover to (Name)	

Staff No : ____ Shift : ____

Date In : ____ Time In : ____ Date Out : ____ Time Out : ____

Hours Worked	
Signature	
Job Description :	
Equipment Condition	
Shift Report	

Action to Complete

No.	Action	Completed Date

Completed Actions

No.	Action	Completed Date

NOTES

_____

CLOSING SHIFT SIGNATURE   STARTING SHIFT SIGNATURE

Year : _____

Month : _____

Day : | M | T | W | T | F | S | S |
|---|---|---|---|---|---|---|
| | | | | | | |

Date : _____

Department	
Staff Name	Rank / Grade	
Supervisor's Name	
Handover Type	
Handover Time	
Handover to (Name)	
Staff No :	Shift :
Date In :	Time In :	Date Out :	Time Out :
Hours Worked	
Signature	
Job Description :	
Equipment Condition	
Shift Report	

Action to Complete

No.	Action	Completed Date

Completed Actions

No.	Action	Completed Date

NOTES

_____
CLOSING SHIFT SIGNATURE

_____
STARTING SHIFT SIGNATURE

Year :

Month :

Day : | M | T | W | T | F | S | S |

Date :

Department	
Staff Name	Rank / Grade
Supervisor's Name	
Handover Type	
Handover Time	
Handover to (Name)	
Staff No :	Shift :
Date In :	Time In :	Date Out :	Time Out :
Hours Worked	
Signature	
Job Description :	
Equipment Condition	
Shift Report	

Action to Complete

No.	Action	Completed Date

Completed Actions

No.	Action	Completed Date

NOTES

CLOSING SHIFT SIGNATURE

STARTING SHIFT SIGNATURE

Year :

Day : | M | T | W | T | F | S | S |
|---|---|---|---|---|---|---|
| | | | | | | |

Month :

Date :

Department	
Staff Name	Rank / Grade
Supervisor's Name	
Handover Type	
Handover Time	
Handover to (Name)	

Staff No :		Shift :	
Date In :	Time In :	Date Out :	Time Out :

Hours Worked	
Signature	
Job Description :	
Equipment Condition	
Shift Report	

Action to Complete

No.	Action	Completed Date

Completed Actions

No.	Action	Completed Date

NOTES

_____ CLOSING SHIFT SIGNATURE

_____ STARTING SHIFT SIGNATURE

Year : _____   Month : _____

Day :

M	T	W	T	F	S	S

Date : _____

Department	
Staff Name	Rank / Grade	
Supervisor's Name	
Handover Type	
Handover Time	
Handover to (Name)	
Staff No :	Shift :
Date In :	Time In :	Date Out :	Time Out :
Hours Worked	
Signature	
Job Description :	
Equipment Condition	
Shift Report	

Action to Complete

No.	Action	Completed Date

Completed Actions

No.	Action	Completed Date

NOTES

_____
_____
_____
_____
_____
_____

CLOSING SHIFT SIGNATURE   **STARTING SHIFT SIGNATURE**

Year :

Day : | M | T | W | T | F | S | S |
|---|---|---|---|---|---|---|
| | | | | | | |

Month :

Date :

Department	
Staff Name	Rank / Grade
Supervisor's Name	
Handover Type	
Handover Time	
Handover to (Name)	
Staff No :	Shift :
Date In :	Time In :	Date Out :	Time Out :
Hours Worked	
Signature	
Job Description :	
Equipment Condition	
Shift Report	

Action to Complete

No.	Action	Completed Date

Completed Actions

No.	Action	Completed Date

─ NOTES ─

CLOSING SHIFT SIGNATURE

STARTING SHIFT SIGNATURE

Year : _____

Month : _____

Day : | M | T | W | T | F | S | S |
|---|---|---|---|---|---|---|
| | | | | | | |

Date : _____

Department	
Staff Name	Rank / Grade
Supervisor's Name	
Handover Type	
Handover Time	
Handover to (Name)	
Staff No :	Shift :
Date In :	Time In :	Date Out :	Time Out :
Hours Worked	
Signature	
Job Description :	
Equipment Condition	
Shift Report	

Action to Complete

No.	Action	Completed Date

Completed Actions

No.	Action	Completed Date

NOTES

CLOSING SHIFT SIGNATURE

STARTING SHIFT SIGNATURE

Year : _____

Day : | M | T | W | T | F | S | S |
|---|---|---|---|---|---|---|
| | | | | | | |

Month : _____

Date : _____

Department	
Staff Name		**Rank / Grade**	
Supervisor's Name	
Handover Type	
Handover Time	
Handover to (Name)	
Staff No :		**Shift :**	
Date In :	**Time In :**	**Date Out :**	**Time Out :**
Hours Worked	
Signature	
Job Description :	
Equipment Condition	
Shift Report	

Action to Complete

No.	Action	Completed Date

Completed Actions

No.	Action	Completed Date

NOTES

_____

_____

CLOSING SHIFT SIGNATURE

STARTING SHIFT SIGNATURE

Year : [ ]

Month : [ ]

Day :

M	T	W	T	F	S	S

Date : [ ]

Department	
Staff Name	Rank / Grade	
Supervisor's Name	
Handover Type	
Handover Time	
Handover to (Name)	
Staff No :	Shift :
Date In :	Time In :	Date Out :	Time Out :
Hours Worked	
Signature	
Job Description :	
Equipment Condition	
Shift Report	

Action to Complete

No.	Action	Completed Date

Completed Actions

No.	Action	Completed Date

NOTES

CLOSING SHIFT SIGNATURE

STARTING SHIFT SIGNATURE

Year :

Month :

Day :

M	T	W	T	F	S	S

Date :

Department	
Staff Name	**Rank / Grade**
Supervisor's Name	
Handover Type	
Handover Time	
Handover to (Name)	
Staff No :	**Shift :**
Date In :	**Time In :** **Date Out :** **Time Out :**
Hours Worked	
Signature	
Job Description :	
Equipment Condition	
Shift Report	

Action to Complete

No.	Action	Completed Date

Completed Actions

No.	Action	Completed Date

NOTES

CLOSING SHIFT SIGNATURE

STARTING SHIFT SIGNATURE

Year :								Month :	
Day :	M	T	W	T	F	S	S	Date :	

Department	
Staff Name	**Rank / Grade**
Supervisor's Name	
Handover Type	
Handover Time	
Handover to (Name)	
Staff No :	**Shift :**
Date In :	**Time In :** **Date Out :** **Time Out :**
Hours Worked	
Signature	
Job Description :	
Equipment Condition	
Shift Report	

Action to Complete

No.	Action	Completed Date

Completed Actions

No.	Action	Completed Date

NOTES

_____
CLOSING SHIFT SIGNATURE

_____
STARTING SHIFT SIGNATURE

Year :

Month :

Day :

M	T	W	T	F	S	S

Date :

Department	
Staff Name	**Rank / Grade**
Supervisor's Name	
Handover Type	
Handover Time	
Handover to (Name)	
Staff No :	**Shift :**
Date In :	**Time In :**	**Date Out :**	**Time Out :**
Hours Worked	
Signature	
Job Description :	
Equipment Condition	
Shift Report	

Action to Complete

No.	Action	Completed Date

Completed Actions

No.	Action	Completed Date

NOTES

CLOSING SHIFT SIGNATURE

STARTING SHIFT SIGNATURE

Year :

Month :

Day :

M	T	W	T	F	S	S

Date :

Department	
Staff Name	**Rank / Grade**
Supervisor's Name	
Handover Type	
Handover Time	
Handover to (Name)	
Staff No :	**Shift :**
Date In :	**Time In :**	**Date Out :**	**Time Out :**
Hours Worked	
Signature	
Job Description :	
Equipment Condition	
Shift Report	

Action to Complete

No.	Action	Completed Date

Completed Actions

No.	Action	Completed Date

NOTES

CLOSING SHIFT SIGNATURE

STARTING SHIFT SIGNATURE

Year :

Day :

M	T	W	T	F	S	S

Month :

Date :

Department	
Staff Name		**Rank / Grade**	
Supervisor's Name	
Handover Type	
Handover Time	
Handover to (Name)	

Staff No :		**Shift :**	
Date In :	**Time In :**	**Date Out :**	**Time Out :**
Hours Worked			
Signature			
Job Description :			
Equipment Condition			
Shift Report			

Action to Complete

No.	Action	Completed Date

Completed Actions

No.	Action	Completed Date

NOTES

_____ CLOSING SHIFT SIGNATURE

_____ STARTING SHIFT SIGNATURE

Year :								Month :	

Day :	M	T	W	T	F	S	S

Date :

Department	
Staff Name	Rank / Grade
Supervisor's Name	
Handover Type	
Handover Time	
Handover to (Name)	

Staff No :		Shift :

Date In :	Time In :	Date Out :	Time Out :

Hours Worked	
Signature	
Job Description :	
Equipment Condition	
Shift Report	

Action to Complete

No.	Action	Completed Date

Completed Actions

No.	Action	Completed Date

NOTES

CLOSING SHIFT SIGNATURE

STARTING SHIFT SIGNATURE

Year : _____

Month : _____

Day :

M	T	W	T	F	S	S

Date : _____

Department	
Staff Name	**Rank / Grade**
Supervisor's Name	
Handover Type	
Handover Time	
Handover to (Name)	

Staff No :		**Shift :**	
Date In :	**Time In :**	**Date Out :**	**Time Out :**

Hours Worked	
Signature	
Job Description :	
Equipment Condition	
Shift Report	

Action to Complete

No.	Action	Completed Date

Completed Actions

No.	Action	Completed Date

NOTES

_____

_____

_____

_____

_____

CLOSING SHIFT SIGNATURE

STARTING SHIFT SIGNATURE

Year : [   ]

Month : [   ]

Day :

M	T	W	T	F	S	S

Date : [   ]

Department	
Staff Name	**Rank / Grade**
Supervisor's Name	
Handover Type	
Handover Time	
Handover to (Name)	
Staff No :	**Shift :**
Date In :	**Time In :** **Date Out :** **Time Out :**
Hours Worked	
Signature	
Job Description :	
Equipment Condition	
Shift Report	

Action to Complete

No.	Action	Completed Date

Completed Actions

No.	Action	Completed Date

— **NOTES** —

_____   _____
CLOSING SHIFT SIGNATURE   **STARTING SHIFT SIGNATURE**

Year :								Month :	
Day :	M	T	W	T	F	S	S	Date :	

Department			
Staff Name		Rank / Grade	
Supervisor's Name			
Handover Type			
Handover Time			
Handover to (Name)			
Staff No :		Shift :	
Date In :	Time In :	Date Out :	Time Out :
Hours Worked			
Signature			
Job Description :			
Equipment Condition			
Shift Report			

Action to Complete			**Completed Actions**		
No.	Action	Completed Date	No.	Action	Completed Date

NOTES

_____
CLOSING SHIFT SIGNATURE

_____
STARTING SHIFT SIGNATURE

Year :

Month :

Day :

M	T	W	T	F	S	S

Date :

Department	
Staff Name	Rank / Grade
Supervisor's Name	
Handover Type	
Handover Time	
Handover to (Name)	
Staff No :	Shift :
Date In :	Time In : Date Out : Time Out :
Hours Worked	
Signature	
Job Description :	
Equipment Condition	
Shift Report	

Action to Complete

No.	Action	Completed Date

Completed Actions

No.	Action	Completed Date

NOTES

CLOSING SHIFT SIGNATURE

STARTING SHIFT SIGNATURE

Year :

Month :

Day :

M	T	W	T	F	S	S

Date :

Department	
Staff Name	**Rank / Grade**
Supervisor's Name	
Handover Type	
Handover Time	
Handover to (Name)	
Staff No :	**Shift :**
Date In : Time In :	Date Out : Time Out :
Hours Worked	
Signature	
Job Description :	
Equipment Condition	
Shift Report	

Action to Complete

No.	Action	Completed Date

Completed Actions

No.	Action	Completed Date

NOTES

_____
CLOSING SHIFT SIGNATURE

_____
STARTING SHIFT SIGNATURE

Year :

Month :

Day :

M	T	W	T	F	S	S

Date :

Department	
Staff Name	**Rank / Grade**
Supervisor's Name	
Handover Type	
Handover Time	
Handover to (Name)	
Staff No :	**Shift :**
Date In :	**Time In :**	**Date Out :**	**Time Out :**
Hours Worked	
Signature	
Job Description :	
Equipment Condition	
Shift Report	

Action to Complete

No.	Action	Completed Date

Completed Actions

No.	Action	Completed Date

NOTES

CLOSING SHIFT SIGNATURE

STARTING SHIFT SIGNATURE

Year :

Month :

Date :

Day :	M	T	W	T	F	S	S

Department	
Staff Name		**Rank / Grade**	
Supervisor's Name	
Handover Type	
Handover Time	
Handover to (Name)	
Staff No :	**Shift :**
Date In :	Time In :	Date Out :	Time Out :
Hours Worked	
Signature	
Job Description :	
Equipment Condition	
Shift Report	

Action to Complete

No.	Action	Completed Date

Completed Actions

No.	Action	Completed Date

NOTES

CLOSING SHIFT SIGNATURE

STARTING SHIFT SIGNATURE

Year :

Month :

Day :

M	T	W	T	F	S	S

Date :

Department	
Staff Name	Rank / Grade
Supervisor's Name	
Handover Type	
Handover Time	
Handover to (Name)	
Staff No :	Shift :
Date In :	Time In : Date Out : Time Out :
Hours Worked	
Signature	
Job Description :	
Equipment Condition	
Shift Report	

Action to Complete

No.	Action	Completed Date

Completed Actions

No.	Action	Completed Date

NOTES

CLOSING SHIFT SIGNATURE

STARTING SHIFT SIGNATURE

Year :

Month :

Day :

M	T	W	T	F	S	S

Date :

Department	
Staff Name	**Rank / Grade**
Supervisor's Name	
Handover Type	
Handover Time	
Handover to (Name)	
Staff No :	**Shift :**
Date In :	**Time In :** / **Date Out :** / **Time Out :**
Hours Worked	
Signature	
Job Description :	
Equipment Condition	
Shift Report	

Action to Complete

No.	Action	Completed Date

Completed Actions

No.	Action	Completed Date

NOTES

CLOSING SHIFT SIGNATURE

STARTING SHIFT SIGNATURE

Year :

Day :

M	T	W	T	F	S	S

Month :

Date :

Department	
Staff Name	**Rank / Grade**
Supervisor's Name	
Handover Type	
Handover Time	
Handover to (Name)	
Staff No :	**Shift :**
Date In :	**Time In :**	**Date Out :**	**Time Out :**
Hours Worked	
Signature	
Job Description :	
Equipment Condition	
Shift Report	

Action to Complete

No.	Action	Completed Date

Completed Actions

No.	Action	Completed Date

NOTES

CLOSING SHIFT SIGNATURE

STARTING SHIFT SIGNATURE

Year : _____

Month : _____

Day : | M | T | W | T | F | S | S |
| | | | | | | |

Date : _____

Department	
Staff Name	Rank / Grade
Supervisor's Name	
Handover Type	
Handover Time	
Handover to (Name)	

Staff No :	Shift :

Date In :	Time In :	Date Out :	Time Out :

Hours Worked	
Signature	
Job Description :	
Equipment Condition	
Shift Report	

Action to Complete

No.	Action	Completed Date

Completed Actions

No.	Action	Completed Date

NOTES

_____
CLOSING SHIFT SIGNATURE

_____
STARTING SHIFT SIGNATURE

Year :

Month :

Day :

M	T	W	T	F	S	S

Date :

Department	
Staff Name	**Rank / Grade**
Supervisor's Name	
Handover Type	
Handover Time	
Handover to (Name)	
Staff No :	**Shift :**
Date In :	**Time In :** / **Date Out :** / **Time Out :**
Hours Worked	
Signature	
Job Description :	
Equipment Condition	
Shift Report	

Action to Complete

No.	Action	Completed Date

Completed Actions

No.	Action	Completed Date

NOTES

CLOSING SHIFT SIGNATURE

STARTING SHIFT SIGNATURE

Year :

Day : M T W T F S S

Month :

Date :

Department	
Staff Name	**Rank / Grade**
Supervisor's Name	
Handover Type	
Handover Time	
Handover to (Name)	
Staff No :	**Shift :**
Date In :	**Time In :**	**Date Out :**	**Time Out :**
Hours Worked	
Signature	
Job Description :	
Equipment Condition	
Shift Report	

Action to Complete

No.	Action	Completed Date

Completed Actions

No.	Action	Completed Date

NOTES

CLOSING SHIFT SIGNATURE

STARTING SHIFT SIGNATURE

Year : |

Day : | M | T | W | T | F | S | S |

Month :

Date :

Department	
Staff Name		Rank / Grade	
Supervisor's Name	
Handover Type	
Handover Time	
Handover to (Name)	
Staff No :		Shift :
Date In :	Time In :	Date Out :	Time Out :
Hours Worked	
Signature	
Job Description :	
Equipment Condition	
Shift Report	

Action to Complete

No.	Action	Completed Date

Completed Actions

No.	Action	Completed Date

NOTES

CLOSING SHIFT SIGNATURE

STARTING SHIFT SIGNATURE

Year :		Month :	

Day : M T W T F S S

Date :	

Department	
Staff Name	Rank / Grade
Supervisor's Name	
Handover Type	
Handover Time	
Handover to (Name)	
Staff No :	Shift :
Date In :	Time In :	Date Out :	Time Out :
Hours Worked	
Signature	
Job Description :	
Equipment Condition	
Shift Report	

Action to Complete

No.	Action	Completed Date

Completed Actions

No.	Action	Completed Date

NOTES

_____
CLOSING SHIFT SIGNATURE

_____
STARTING SHIFT SIGNATURE

Year :

Day : | M | T | W | T | F | S | S |

Month :

Date :

Department	
Staff Name	Rank / Grade	
Supervisor's Name	
Handover Type	
Handover Time	
Handover to (Name)	
Staff No :	Shift :
Date In :	Time In :	Date Out :	Time Out :
Hours Worked	
Signature	
Job Description :	
Equipment Condition	
Shift Report	

Action to Complete

No.	Action	Completed Date

Completed Actions

No.	Action	Completed Date

NOTES

CLOSING SHIFT SIGNATURE

STARTING SHIFT SIGNATURE

Year :

Month :

Day : | M | T | W | T | F | S | S |
|---|---|---|---|---|---|---|
| | | | | | | |

Date :

Department	
Staff Name		Rank / Grade	
Supervisor's Name	
Handover Type	
Handover Time	
Handover to (Name)	
Staff No :		Shift :	
Date In :	Time In :	Date Out :	Time Out :
Hours Worked	
Signature	
Job Description :	
Equipment Condition	
Shift Report	

Action to Complete

No.	Action	Completed Date

Completed Actions

No.	Action	Completed Date

NOTES

_____   _____

CLOSING SHIFT SIGNATURE   **STARTING SHIFT SIGNATURE**

HANDOVER LOG

Year :

Month :

Day : | M | T | W | T | F | S | S |

Date :

Department	
Staff Name	**Rank / Grade**
Supervisor's Name	
Handover Type	
Handover Time	
Handover to (Name)	
Staff No :	**Shift :**
Date In :	**Time In :**	**Date Out :**	**Time Out :**
Hours Worked	
Signature	
Job Description :	
Equipment Condition	
Shift Report	

Action to Complete

No.	Action	Completed Date

Completed Actions

No.	Action	Completed Date

NOTES

_____
CLOSING SHIFT SIGNATURE

_____
STARTING SHIFT SIGNATURE

Year :

Month :

Day : | M | T | W | T | F | S | S |

Date :

Department	
Staff Name	**Rank / Grade**
Supervisor's Name	
Handover Type	
Handover Time	
Handover to (Name)	
Staff No :	**Shift :**
Date In :	**Time In :**	**Date Out :**	**Time Out :**
Hours Worked	
Signature	
Job Description :	
Equipment Condition	
Shift Report	

Action to Complete

No.	Action	Completed Date

Completed Actions

No.	Action	Completed Date

NOTES

___

CLOSING SHIFT SIGNATURE   **STARTING SHIFT SIGNATURE**

Year :								Month :	
Day :	M	T	W	T	F	S	S	Date :	

Department		
Staff Name	**Rank / Grade**	
Supervisor's Name		
Handover Type		
Handover Time		
Handover to (Name)		
Staff No :	**Shift :**	
Date In :	**Time In :**	**Date Out :**	**Time Out :**
Hours Worked		
Signature		
Job Description :		
Equipment Condition		
Shift Report		

Action to Complete			Completed Actions		
No.	Action	Completed Date	No.	Action	Completed Date

NOTES

CLOSING SHIFT SIGNATURE   **STARTING SHIFT SIGNATURE**

Year :

Month :

Day :

M	T	W	T	F	S	S

Date :

Department

Staff Name

Rank / Grade

Supervisor's Name

Handover Type

Handover Time

Handover to (Name)

Staff No :

Shift :

Date In :

Time In :

Date Out :

Time Out :

Hours Worked

Signature

Job Description :

Equipment Condition

Shift Report

Action to Complete			Completed Actions		
No.	Action	Completed Date	No.	Action	Completed Date

NOTES

CLOSING SHIFT SIGNATURE

STARTING SHIFT SIGNATURE

Year : _____

Month : _____

Day : | M | T | W | T | F | S | S |
|---|---|---|---|---|---|---|
| | | | | | | |

Date : _____

Department	
Staff Name	Rank / Grade
Supervisor's Name	
Handover Type	
Handover Time	
Handover to (Name)	

Staff No :		Shift :	
Date In :	Time In :	Date Out :	Time Out :

Hours Worked	
Signature	
Job Description :	
Equipment Condition	
Shift Report	

Action to Complete

No.	Action	Completed Date

Completed Actions

No.	Action	Completed Date

— NOTES —

_____
_____
_____
_____
_____
_____

CLOSING SHIFT SIGNATURE   **STARTING SHIFT SIGNATURE**

HANDOVER LOG

Year :								Month :		
Day :	M	T	W	T	F	S	S	Date :		

Department	
Staff Name	

	Rank / Grade	

Supervisor's Name	
Handover Type	
Handover Time	
Handover to (Name)	

Staff No :		Shift :	
Date In :	Time In :	Date Out :	Time Out :

Hours Worked	
Signature	
Job Description :	
Equipment Condition	
Shift Report	

Action to Complete

No.	Action	Completed Date

Completed Actions

No.	Action	Completed Date

NOTES

CLOSING SHIFT SIGNATURE   STARTING SHIFT SIGNATURE

Year :

Day : | M | T | W | T | F | S | S |

Month :

Date :

Department	
Staff Name	Rank / Grade
Supervisor's Name	
Handover Type	
Handover Time	
Handover to (Name)	
Staff No :	Shift :
Date In :	Time In :	Date Out :	Time Out :
Hours Worked	
Signature	
Job Description :	
Equipment Condition	
Shift Report	

Action to Complete

No.	Action	Completed Date

Completed Actions

No.	Action	Completed Date

NOTES

CLOSING SHIFT SIGNATURE

STARTING SHIFT SIGNATURE

Year :

Month :

Day :

M	T	W	T	F	S	S

Date :

Department	
Staff Name		**Rank / Grade**	
Supervisor's Name	
Handover Type	
Handover Time	
Handover to (Name)	
Staff No :		**Shift :**	
Date In :	**Time In :**	**Date Out :**	**Time Out :**
Hours Worked	
Signature	
Job Description :	
Equipment Condition	
Shift Report	

Action to Complete

No.	Action	Completed Date

Completed Actions

No.	Action	Completed Date

NOTES

CLOSING SHIFT SIGNATURE

STARTING SHIFT SIGNATURE

Year : _____

Month : _____

Day : | M | T | W | T | F | S | S |
|---|---|---|---|---|---|---|
| | | | | | | |

Date : _____

Department	
Staff Name		Rank / Grade	
Supervisor's Name	
Handover Type	
Handover Time	
Handover to (Name)	
Staff No :		Shift :	
Date In :	Time In :	Date Out :	Time Out :
Hours Worked	
Signature	
Job Description :	
Equipment Condition	
Shift Report	

Action to Complete

No.	Action	Completed Date

Completed Actions

No.	Action	Completed Date

NOTES

_____

_____

_____

_____

_____

_____

CLOSING SHIFT SIGNATURE   **STARTING SHIFT SIGNATURE**

Year :	Month :
Day : M T W T F S S	Date :

Department			
Staff Name		Rank / Grade	
Supervisor's Name			
Handover Type			
Handover Time			
Handover to (Name)			
Staff No :		Shift :	
Date In :	Time In :	Date Out :	Time Out :
Hours Worked			
Signature			
Job Description :			
Equipment Condition			
Shift Report			

Action to Complete

No.	Action	Completed Date

Completed Actions

No.	Action	Completed Date

NOTES

CLOSING SHIFT SIGNATURE   STARTING SHIFT SIGNATURE

Year :								Month :	
Day :	M	T	W	T	F	S	S		
								Date :	

Department	
Staff Name	Rank / Grade
Supervisor's Name	
Handover Type	
Handover Time	
Handover to (Name)	
Staff No :	Shift :
Date In :	Time In :	Date Out :	Time Out :
Hours Worked	
Signature	
Job Description :	
Equipment Condition	
Shift Report	

Action to Complete

No.	Action	Completed Date

Completed Actions

No.	Action	Completed Date

NOTES

CLOSING SHIFT SIGNATURE   STARTING SHIFT SIGNATURE

Year :

Month :

Day :

M	T	W	T	F	S	S

Date :

Department	
Staff Name	**Rank / Grade**
Supervisor's Name	
Handover Type	
Handover Time	
Handover to (Name)	
Staff No :	**Shift :**
Date In :	**Time In :**	**Date Out :**	**Time Out :**
Hours Worked	
Signature	
Job Description :	
Equipment Condition	
Shift Report	

Action to Complete

No.	Action	Completed Date

Completed Actions

No.	Action	Completed Date

NOTES

_____
CLOSING SHIFT SIGNATURE

_____
STARTING SHIFT SIGNATURE

Year :

Day : | M | T | W | T | F | S | S |

Month :

Date :

Department

Staff Name | **Rank / Grade**

Supervisor's Name

Handover Type

Handover Time

Handover to (Name)

Staff No : | **Shift :**

Date In : | Time In : | Date Out : | Time Out :

Hours Worked

Signature

Job Description :

Equipment Condition

Shift Report

Action to Complete

No.	Action	Completed Date

Completed Actions

No.	Action	Completed Date

NOTES

CLOSING SHIFT SIGNATURE   **STARTING SHIFT SIGNATURE**

Year :		Month :	

Day : | M | T | W | T | F | S | S |
|---|---|---|---|---|---|---|
| | | | | | | |

Date :

Department	
Staff Name		Rank / Grade	
Supervisor's Name	
Handover Type	
Handover Time	
Handover to (Name)	
Staff No :	Shift :
Date In :	Time In :	Date Out :	Time Out :
Hours Worked	
Signature	
Job Description :	
Equipment Condition	
Shift Report	

Action to Complete

No.	Action	Completed Date

Completed Actions

No.	Action	Completed Date

NOTES

CLOSING SHIFT SIGNATURE

STARTING SHIFT SIGNATURE

Year :

Day : | M | T | W | T | F | S | S |
|---|---|---|---|---|---|---|
| | | | | | | |

Month :

Date :

Department	
Staff Name	Rank / Grade
Supervisor's Name	
Handover Type	
Handover Time	
Handover to (Name)	
Staff No :	Shift :
Date In :	Time In :	Date Out :	Time Out :
Hours Worked	
Signature	
Job Description :	
Equipment Condition	
Shift Report	

Action to Complete

No.	Action	Completed Date

Completed Actions

No.	Action	Completed Date

NOTES

_____ CLOSING SHIFT SIGNATURE

_____ STARTING SHIFT SIGNATURE

Year : _____

Month : _____

Day :

M	T	W	T	F	S	S

Date : _____

Department	
Staff Name	**Rank / Grade**
Supervisor's Name	
Handover Type	
Handover Time	
Handover to (Name)	
Staff No :	**Shift :**
Date In :	**Time In :**	**Date Out :**	**Time Out :**
Hours Worked	
Signature	
Job Description :	
Equipment Condition	
Shift Report	

Action to Complete

No.	Action	Completed Date

Completed Actions

No.	Action	Completed Date

NOTES

_____

CLOSING SHIFT SIGNATURE

STARTING SHIFT SIGNATURE

Year :

Day :

M	T	W	T	F	S	S

Month :

Date :

Department	
Staff Name	**Rank / Grade**
Supervisor's Name	
Handover Type	
Handover Time	
Handover to (Name)	
Staff No :	**Shift :**
Date In :	Time In :	Date Out :	Time Out :
Hours Worked	
Signature	
Job Description :	
Equipment Condition	
Shift Report	

Action to Complete

No.	Action	Completed Date

Completed Actions

No.	Action	Completed Date

NOTES

CLOSING SHIFT SIGNATURE

STARTING SHIFT SIGNATURE

Year : _____

Month : _____

Day :

M	T	W	T	F	S	S

Date : _____

Department	
Staff Name	**Rank / Grade**
Supervisor's Name	
Handover Type	
Handover Time	
Handover to (Name)	
Staff No :	**Shift :**
Date In :	**Time In :** / **Date Out :** / **Time Out :**
Hours Worked	
Signature	
Job Description :	
Equipment Condition	
Shift Report	

Action to Complete

No.	Action	Completed Date

Completed Actions

No.	Action	Completed Date

NOTES

_____

CLOSING SHIFT SIGNATURE

STARTING SHIFT SIGNATURE

Year :

Month :

Day : | M | T | W | T | F | S | S |

Date :

Department	
Staff Name	Rank / Grade
Supervisor's Name	
Handover Type	
Handover Time	
Handover to (Name)	
Staff No :	Shift :
Date In :	Time In :	Date Out :	Time Out :
Hours Worked	
Signature	
Job Description :	
Equipment Condition	
Shift Report	

Action to Complete

No.	Action	Completed Date

Completed Actions

No.	Action	Completed Date

NOTES

CLOSING SHIFT SIGNATURE

STARTING SHIFT SIGNATURE

Made in the USA
Coppell, TX
13 October 2023